pocket: *adjective:* small enoug
issue: *noun:* a vital or unsettle

Designed for our time-presse
pithy handbooks pull together
biggest challenges facing our world – delivering the facts ...
an independent and quick-to-digest format.

Praise for Pocket Issue:

'A brilliant wheeze: the essence of the debate in a very approachable format.' Harriet Lane, The Observer

'Exactly what any busy person needs – the facts at your fingertips! Never get caught out again when a conversation starts on the big issues of our time.' Jeremy Vine, BBC Radio 2 and Panorama

'For everyone who longs to be well-informed but lacks the time (or attention span).' Alex Clark, The Observer

'Prep yourself by keeping the one on global warming in the downstairs loo...' Mary Killen, The Spectator

'Precisely what's needed...' Hephzibah Anderson, The Daily Mail

Dig deeper on any issue we cover through our blog, plus find out about new publications and special offers on our website, www.pocketissue.com. And tell us what you think, we always welcome your suggestions and comments.

Now available in Audio – order online at www.talkingissues.com

Pocket issue
Small briefs for a big world

The Credit Crunch...
how safe is your money?

Published by Pocket Issue, London
www.pocketissue.com
info@pocketissue.com

Copyright © Pocket Issue, 2008
First edition, published July 2008.

ISBN: 0-9554415-6-0
ISBN: 978-0-9554415-6-1

Design by Studio 176.
info@studio176.co.uk

Production by Francois Weideman.
www.writedesign.co.za

Pocket
ISSUE

Each Pocket Issue follows a similar format and for **The Credit Crunch: how safe is your money?** we would like to thank the following team:

Author: Simon Nixon
Illustration: Andrzej Krauze
Production design: Francois Weideman
Editorial: Mary Alexander, Katrina Forde

We would also like to thank those who have offered help and advice along the way:
Merryn Somerset Webb, Constantine Courcoulas, Joanna Everard, Julia Bullock, Nick Band, Flo Bayley, Dr Jonathan Parry, Richard Sunderland, Adam Goodison and Nathaniel Price.

The Pocket Issue Team

Contents

One minute guide

The issues in the blink of an eye

It has a new ring to it and it's often in the headlines, but do you know what the term Credit Crunch really means? How it might affect you on a personal level, and the implications for the economy as a whole? Just one minute to spare? Read on for the pertinent points.

Credit crunch. The credit crunch started in August 2007. The term refers to the sudden contraction of credit across the financial system as banks became increasingly reluctant to lend. It has left individuals and companies facing potentially higher interest costs, or struggling to get access to credit at all.

Subprime mortgages. The credit crunch was triggered by a slump in the US housing market, as a result of rising defaults by so-called subprime borrowers – typically people on low incomes with poor credit histories. As interest rates rose and introductory teaser rates reset, the pace of defaults picked up.

Securitisation. Subprime mortgages proliferated thanks to securitisation – a process that enabled banks to parcel up loans, slice them and dice them and sell them on, so that risks were supposedly spread. As the scale of the subprime losses became clear, banks became increasingly reluctant to lend to one another.

Bank failures. One of the first victims of the credit crunch was Northern Rock, the Newcastle-based lender, which relied on the money markets for the bulk of its funding. It collapsed in August 2007. Two German banks also had to be rescued as a result of the crisis, showing how global the markets had become.

Turning point? The collapse of Bear Stearns was a pivotal

moment in the credit crunch. Had it not been rescued by JP Morgan, other banks might have failed, leading to the collapse of much of the financial system. Since then some markets have recovered but conditions in the real economy are getting worse.

Housing woes. US house prices had fallen 15% by the end of May, the first nationwide fall since the Great Depression. The UK housing market is widely forecast to fall up to 10% in 2008. Other countries that experienced major housing bubbles include Spain and Ireland.

More trouble to come? Other sources of potential losses for the banks include credit card debt, student loans, car loans and rising defaults by highly indebted companies, particularly those backed by private equity.

Helpful central banks. Central banks have provided emergency funding for banks and have cut interest rates to ease the pressure on borrowers. But they must balance action to ease the credit crisis against the risk of moral hazard - encouraging risky behaviour in the future - and the need to guard against rising inflation.

Healthier banks. Banks were slow to face up to their problems but most have since come clean about their exposure to problem mortgage securities and have raised new capital. That gives them a buffer to absorb future losses. But will it be enough if the economy tips into recession?

Not safe yet. The International Monetary Fund reckons total losses to the banking system as a result of the crisis are likely to reach $1 trillion. By the end of May 2008, losses had only reached $386bn.

So the coffee is being passed around and your host is looking serene. Here are some things you should (and shouldn't) say to keep your place at the table.

Have a second helping:

Who was it that said 'Never a borrower or a lender be'? Because it sounds like good old-fashioned advice to me.

Austerity chic is the latest fashion trend. I've taken a sabbatical from clothes shopping. It's better for my bank balance and since I'm consuming less, the environment wins too.

Luckily I've been saving for a rainy day, because I think it might be time to put the umbrella up.

Get your coat:

"Credit crunch" – is that a new kind of chocolate bar? Does it have nuts? Is it wheat-free?

"Bank run?" How many miles are you doing and who are you raising money for? I hope you've got a decent pair of trainers and a sports bra.

People love nothing more than a crisis!

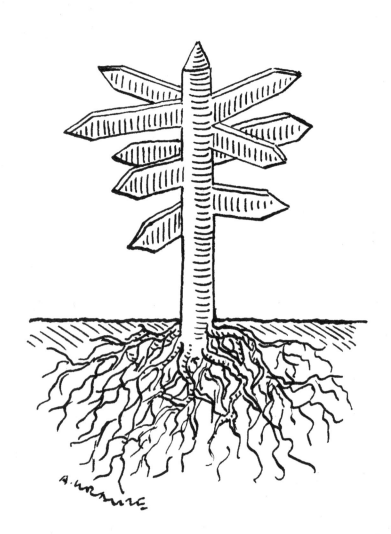

Roots

The important questions answered

The credit crunch – an introduction

It is already being dubbed the worst financial crisis since the Great Depression. What started with falling house prices in America has so far led to the collapse of Northern Rock and Bear Stearns, hundreds of billions of dollars of losses in the global financial system, falling house prices in the US and Britain and talk of recession. How did this crisis come about? How much worse could it get? And what does it mean for our own finances?

What is meant by a "credit crunch"? It refers to the steady withdrawal of credit from the economy so that it becomes harder and more expensive for individuals and companies to borrow. In the UK, the credit crunch has led to the withdrawal of thousands of cheap mortgage deals and a big jump in borrowing costs, leading to fears that many people won't be able to pay their mortgages. Since credit is the lifeblood of the financial system, a credit crunch can have a profound effect on economic activity.

What caused the credit crunch? The initial trigger was a downturn in the US housing market in 2006. By early 2007, the downturn was starting to spark big losses for many US banks who responded by cutting back their mortgage lending, putting further pressure on house prices and triggering more losses. By the middle of 2007, banks became so alarmed at the scale of the losses that they virtually stopped lending to one another. The global banking system has been in deep trouble ever since.

UK personal debt rose 137% between 1999 and 2007

What makes this crisis so serious? There is too much potentially risky debt sloshing around the financial system - much of it owed by individuals. In the US, total credit rose on average 9% a year between 2001 and 2007 to $13.8bn, far outstripping the rate of GDP growth. In the UK, personal debt rose 137% between 1999 and 2007, reaching £1.3 trillion, and in the process exceeding GDP for the first time.

Why were people able to get so deep in debt? Because credit became much more widely available. Not so long ago, only those with impeccable financial histories and steady jobs could get a mortgage or a credit card or a bank overdraft; but during the boom, almost anyone could, often without even having to offer proof of income. For the most part all the borrowing and spending seemed to be good for the economy. The more people splashed out on cars and restaurants and home improvements, the faster the economy grew, the richer they became and the more they could borrow. But now the cheap money has run out, the economy is slowing, and many are struggling to manage huge debts.

How big was this credit bubble? By 2007, the average Briton owed 162% of his annual income, the average American 142%, while the average German owed a comparatively miserly 109%. Meanwhile, savings rates - the proportion of income saved - fell through the floor. The US savings rate turned negative in 2006 for the first time since 1933 at the lowest point of the Great Depression. By 2008, the UK saving rate was 1.1%, the lowest level since 1959, down from 3% in 2007.

UK outstanding mortgage debt currently stands at £1.1 trillion

What form did all this borrowing take? Much of it was accounted for by mortgages. In the US, mortgage debt grew by 119% between 2000 and 2008 to $10.7 trillion. In the UK, outstanding mortgage debt currently stands at £1.1 trillion. But unsecured borrowing, which includes credit card debt, car finance and student loans, also ballooned. In the UK, it hit £220bn - equivalent to £9,000 for every household. By 2007, the UK accounted for two-thirds of all European credit card debt.

In the US, outstanding credit card debt at the end of 2007 stood at just under $1 trillion.

Was all the borrowing by individuals? No. Debt levels soared throughout the financial system. Hedge funds and private equity firms emerged as the dominant players in the markets, taking advantage of cheap, borrowed money to juice up the returns on their investments. So much money poured into private equity that in 2007 they were able to mount bids for some of Britain's biggest companies, including Boots and J. Sainsbury.

Where did all the money come from? Much of it came from developing countries such as China, India and Russia, whose governments and emerging middle classes accumulated vast savings that they ploughed back into Western government bonds. That helped keep western currencies strong and interest rates low – perfect conditions for borrowing. The flipside was that the US and UK sucked in imports, creating huge trade deficits of 7% and 5% of GDP respectively.

The boom

What caused the boom? This was a global phenomenon, largely fuelled by globalisation, which flooded the developed world with cheap goods. That kept inflation down in the West, allowing central banks to keep interest rates low for a long time. The longer this period of stability and rising prosperity continued, the more confident people became and the bigger financial risks they took, while banks relaxed their lending standards.

How big was the house price bubble? Several countries around the world experienced massive housing bubbles, with the biggest house price gains in the US, UK, Australia, Ireland and Spain.

House prices in the US rose 140% between 1997 and 2007. The total value of the US housing market peaked in 2006 at 159% of GDP - the highest since the 1930s.

Much of the demand came from buy-to-let investors relying on rent to pay their mortgages

How big was the housing boom in the UK? In the UK, the housing boom was even more spectacular. House prices trebled over the same period. By mid-2007, the average home cost a record six times the average wage, compared to a long-term average of 3.7 times, according to Capital Economics. As first time buyers were increasingly priced out of the market, much of the demand came from buy-to-let investors relying on rent to pay their mortgages.

Was it just house prices that were affected? No. A tide of money flowed into commercial property, such as office blocks and shopping centres, and yields in many cases actually fell below the yield on government debt. At the peak of the boom, HSBC sold its Canary Wharf tower for £1.09bn. At that price, its rental income yielded just 3.8% - which was far less than the 5.75% you could earn from putting your money in the bank.

What about other investments? Easy credit pushed up the prices of almost every kind of asset. Corporate bond prices soared, pushing down yields so that spreads - the difference in yield over government bonds - fell to record lows. Commodity prices - gold, oil, and base metals - also rocketed. More exotic investments such as fine wine and modern art were caught in the frenzy.

In the summer of 2007, a group of investors paid $100m for a diamond-encrusted skull created by the British artist Damien Hirst.

How about the stock market? Share prices were less affected by the credit bubble, largely because they were still recovering from the earlier stock market bubble at the end of the Nineties. Even so, a debt-fuelled private equity takeover boom helped push shares higher. The private equity firms were themselves benefiting from an extraordinary loosening of credit standards that saw many of the covenants designed to protect lenders dropped from loans to create so-called "covenant-lite" loans.

Average wages grew only 4% and income inequality rose to the highest level since the Victorian age

Did everyone do well out of the boom? In the space of little more than 20 years, the number of people in The Sunday Times Rich list who had made their own money as opposed to inherited it rose from 25% to 75%. By 2007, Britain boasted 75 billionaires. But for the average Briton, the boom was less kind. Average wages grew only 4% and income inequality rose to the highest level since the Victorian age.

The bust

Why did the boom come to an end in 2007? Because millions of US homeowners who had been lured into the housing market with cheap introductory "teaser" rates on their mortgage deals were suddenly faced with a sharp rise in their monthly interest bills. US interest rates, which had been cut to just 1% in the aftermath of the dotcom crash, started to rise again in 2004 and by 2006 had reached 5.25%. Many homeowners saw their bills soar and were unable to pay, causing their homes to be repossessed.

How bad is the situation in the US housing market? By the end of April 2008, the average house price in the US had fallen by 12.7%. In the worst hit areas such as Florida and California prices in some neighbourhoods have fallen by more than 30%.

Capital Economics predicts UK house prices will fall 8% in 2008 and 10% in 2009

How far has the crisis spread? The crisis is worst in countries that experienced the biggest house price bubbles: the UK, Spain, Ireland and Australia. In the UK, by the end of April 2008 house prices nationally had fallen by a modest 1% from their peak, but all forecasters now predict much steeper falls. Capital Economics predicts prices will fall 8% in 2008 and 10% in 2009.

How big have the losses been so far? By the end of May 2008, banks around the world had written off a combined $380bn, most of it on US mortgages. The IMF forecasts that by the end of the crisis, banks will have been forced to write off up to $1 trillion.

Who have been the biggest casualties? Two major banks have already collapsed as a result of the credit crisis. Northern Rock, the UK mortgage lender, was an early casualty in September 2007. It was initially bailed out by the Bank of England until finally being nationalised in March 2008. The other major casualty was Bear Stearns, the fifth largest US investment bank, which was rescued by JP Morgan in a deal that valued the bank at just 6.5% of its market value a year earlier.

Which other banks have been affected? Most of the losses so far have been concentrated among US banks, in particular the investment banks, such as Citigroup, Merrill Lynch, Morgan Stanley and Lehman Brothers. Some European banks have also been hard hit, including the Swiss banks UBS and Credit Suisse and the UK's Royal Bank of Scotland. So far, the other British banks, such as Barclays, Lloyds TSB and HBOS have not yet had to write off large sums, but if the UK housing market continues to deteriorate, that may change.

The credit crunch - the issues

A credit crunch is the process by which credit is rapidly withdrawn from the financial system, forcing banks to cut back on lending and pushing up interest rates.

The current credit crisis comes at the end of a long boom that was marked by huge house price bubbles in the US, UK, Spain, Ireland and Australia.

The crisis was triggered by problems in the US housing market, which first started to fall in 2006, leading to rising defaults and losses for the banks.

By mid-2007, the losses in the banking system had become so large that banks stopped lending to each other, either because they had problems of their own, or they did not trust each other.

Northern Rock was forced to turn to the Bank of England after being unable to roll over existing funding, triggering the first run on a UK bank for 140 years.

By the end of April, the world's biggest banks had written off more than $350bn in bad debts. The IMF reckons the total losses on US mortgages could reach $1 trillion.

Bear Stearns, which collapsed in March, was Wall Street's fifth largest investment bank. JP Morgan rescued it for a tiny fraction of its value a year earlier.

The subprime mortgage debacle

The credit crunch was triggered by the collapse of the US housing market. House prices in the US soared during the boom, fuelled by a long period of ultra-low interest rates. At the heart of the boom were the now notorious subprime mortgages. When the bubble burst, these borrowers were the first to be affected - with disastrous consequences.

What are subprime mortgages? Subprime mortgages are home loans made to people who were considered a high credit risk, either because they had a poor credit history, or because they had a low and irregular income and very few savings for a deposit. The worst subprime mortgages were sometimes referred to as Ninja mortgages - no income, no job or assets. These borrowers would often be lured into buying homes with offers of loans for 100% or more of their value and very low "teaser" rates that kept monthly payments affordable for an initial period, but then "reset" to a higher interest rate later on.

In some poorer districts subprime accounts for more than 40% of all new mortgages

How big was the subprime mortgage market? By the middle of 2007, it accounted for 10% of all US mortgages, or a combined total of $1.3 trillion of loans. But that doesn't give the full picture. In some poorer districts, including parts of Florida, Ohio and Los Angeles, subprime accounted for more than 40% of all new mortgages. In some of these areas, house prices have now fallen more than 30% and local estate agents offer prospective buyers ghoulish tours through boarded-up neighbourhoods of empty homes.

Why have prices fallen so far? Thanks to a big rise in US interest rates, those mortgages whose teaser rates expired towards the end of 2006 started to reset at much higher rates - typically 25-30% higher. Many borrowers simply defaulted. Repossessions were running 90% higher in early 2008 compared to a year earlier. Now, with few buyers around, banks are forced to sell the houses for a fraction of their original value - and in doing so, drag down the value of neighbouring properties.

How much money is at stake? At the end of February 2008, 8.8m mortgage holders, or 17% of the US total, were in negative equity - in other words, their home loans were worth more than the value of the house. At that point, house prices had fallen 9% from their peak. If prices fall a further 10%, that figure will rise to 14m homeowners in negative equity. And with the average mortgage worth $225,000, that suggests a potential $3 trillion problem.

This has raised fears of an avalanche of "jingle mail"

Does everyone with negative equity default? Historically, no. Most try to hang on to their homes. But what is different this time is that, during the boom, banks dished out mortgages with much higher loan to value ratios: loans worth 100% of the value of the home were widespread. This has raised fears of an avalanche of "jingle mail" - homeowners with negative equity sending the keys to their homes back to the lender by post. By the end of May 2008, 25% of all subprime mortgages outstanding were in default.

Why did the banks make these loans? Partly because they thought house prices would continue to rise, so that if a buyer got into trouble, there was a good chance the house would by then be worth more than he paid for it. This gave the bank a buffer in case it had to sell at a knockdown price. The assumption that house prices would keep rising seemed to be born out by recent

US economic history, which showed prices had risen almost without interruption since the 1930s. But the other reason banks offered these subprime mortgages is that they did not believe they would be the ones left with the risk thanks to a process known as securitisation, which enabled them to parcel up the mortgages and sell them on.

Securitisation

How does securitisation work? Securitisation is the process by which banks turn ordinary loans into tradable securities - in other words bonds. The interest paid by homeowners on their mortgages is used to pay the interest - or coupon, as it's called - on the bonds. The advantage of this from the bank's point of view is that by selling off the mortgages, possibly at a profit, it can pocket fat fees from arranging the bond issue, while freeing up capital to make a bunch of new loans.

What does this mean for homeowners? Nothing. They continue to make their repayments to the bank as before. But instead of the bank keeping the cash, it pays it on to the bondholders. The difference is that if the homeowner defaults, it is not the bank that suffers the loss but the bondholder.

Why did bondholders want to take this risk? Not all of them did. What securitisation allowed the banks to do was to create different types of bonds depending on different investors' willingness to take risk. The banks did this by slicing up the package of mortgages and issuing the bonds in tranches according to the risk of default. The principle was similar to a line of infantry in an old-fashioned army. If there were problems with the mortgages, the first tranche acted as the first line of defence and took the hit. When these had been wiped out, the second tranche would be exposed and so on. The first tranches carried a higher coupon to compensate for the greater risk. But assuming the banks got their sums right, the chances of the senior tranches being hit by losses were extremely slim so they paid a much lower coupon.

A credit rating of BBB or below is considered high-risk or "non-investment grade"

Who helped this slicing and dicing? The key players in this process were ratings agencies, such as Standard & Poors, Moody's, and Fitch. They provide investors with credit analysis, based on their assessment of the probability that a particular bond will default. Their conclusions are expressed in a credit rating. The highest possible credit rating is AAA, which is awarded to only the most creditworthy issuers, such as the world's richest countries and just 36 of the world's most powerful companies. A credit rating of BBB or below is considered high-risk or "non-investment grade".

What ratings did subprime mortgage bonds attract? Many were rated AAA, putting them on a par with US government bonds. This was because the credit ratings considered it inconceivable that more than, say, 30%, of the mortgages in a given package were likely to default. That meant that 70% of the bonds issued under that securitisation could be considered - literally - as safe as houses.

Why did the rating agencies get it so wrong? The rating agencies came to these conclusions by examining the behaviour of previous borrowers. That showed borrowers had always been able to remortgage at a lower rate when their teaser rates expired, so default rates even among subprime borrowers were low. And since house prices had risen almost without interruption in the US since the 1930s, they assumed that if borrowers did run into trouble, the banks would be able to sell the house for more than the value of the mortgage.

The investors

Who bought these mortgage bonds? Banks and hedge funds were amongst the biggest buyers. They bought the bonds using borrowed money and pocketed the "spread" between the yield on the bonds and the cost of borrowing. Since the spread was typically very small, it required huge sums of borrowed money to make the trade worthwhile. But this also meant that if the underlying assets fell even by a small amount, the fund would be wiped out. This is what happened in August 2007.

Who were the lenders? One of the biggest sources of funding for investors in subprime mortgages turned out to be the Commercial Paper (CP) market. The CP market is like a high interest bank account for big organisations. It is a form of short-term debt, often issued by banks, and typically bought by companies, local authorities and anyone else with large amounts of cash sitting around. Many banks set up separate entities known as structured investment vehicles (SIVs) and conduits to buy up vast amounts of mortgage securities, which they then financed using short-term CP. The banks would provide the SIV or conduit with a guarantee to provide funding if there was a crisis. The advantage of this structure for the banks was that they did not have to put it on their own balance sheet, which meant regulators could not see how much risk they were taking.

The US subprime crisis had become global and spread to the banks

What happened to these funds? They collapsed. During the first half of 2007, the default rate on US subprime mortgages began to pick up. Investors started to get nervous and the prices started to fall. In June, the slide in the price of subprime mortgages was enough to wipe out two huge hedge funds run by Bear Stearns. The US bank stepped in to rescue one of the funds, but allowed the other one to go to the wall. The banks that had lent it money seized the assets and tried to sell them.

What did that do to subprime mortgages? It pushed down the prices further. By early August, panic broke out in the subprime mortgage market so that the French bank BNP Paribas was forced to stop people taking their money out of two of its funds because it could no longer value its assets to say what the fund was worth. Meanwhile, the CP market had effectively shut down, leading to the collapse of a giant conduit managed by an obscure German bank, IKB. The US subprime crisis had become global and spread to the banks.

Why were the banks in trouble? Because they suddenly found themselves being called upon to honour guarantees to conduits and SIVs that they never expected to be called on. Fearing the impact of the sudden dumping of hundreds of billions of dollars of assets of dubious value on their balance sheets, the banks stopped lending to one another, concerned for their own and each other's solvency.

Was this the only problem facing banks? No. The subprime mortgage crisis brought an abrupt end to a private equity takeover frenzy. As a result, banks were left with around $300bn of loans stuck on their balance sheets. These were also supposed to be securitised and parcelled out to investors. But with the credit markets effectively shut, the loans proved impossible to shift, so the banks found themselves even more stretched.

Banks have so far been forced to write off $386bn as a result of the subprime debacle

The damage

How much has the subprime crisis cost so far? The banks have so far been forced to write off $386bn as a result of the subprime debacle. Some of these losses reflect actual losses as a result of foreclosures on bad loans. The rest reflect the fall in the value of mortgage securities as the market tries to work out what the ultimate bill might be. Many triple A-rated US subprime securities are now trading at just 10 cents in the dollar, which suggests the market thinks that the entire package of loans will ultimately prove worthless.

Is the damage limited to US subprime? No. As the credit crunch has continued, cracks have started to emerge in supposedly better quality US mortgages. Meanwhile, the UK house price bubble has also burst, putting at risk more than £300bn of UK mortgage securities.

Subprime – the issues

What will be the ultimate losses from the subprime debacle? The IMF has estimated that total losses may ultimately come to $1 trillion.

Subprime mortgages are loans made to people with poor credit histories or who have little or no deposit to put on their house or who are otherwise considered uncreditworthy.

At the peak of the boom, subprime mortgages accounted for 10% of all US mortgage lending. In some districts in Florida, Ohio and California, it accounted for as much as 40%.

The banks were willing to make these loans because they did not expect to hold on to them for long but to sell them on to investors in the form of securities.

The ratings agencies played a key role in the crisis by awarding many mortgage securities the highest possible triple A rating that subsequently proved to be worthless.

The biggest buyers of mortgage securities were banks and hedge funds who financed their purchases using large amounts of borrowed money.

When the subprime losses started mounting, the value of the securities fell, causing problems for the funds that owned them and could no longer repay their lenders.

The banks were forced to take on to their own balance sheets large portfolios of assets under the terms of guarantees they never expected to have to honour.

This put huge strain in bank balance sheets. As a result, they stopped lending to one another.

Bubbles – past and present

At the heart of the current financial crisis was both a bubble in housing in a number of countries including the US and UK, plus a global credit bubble that saw yields on mortgage bonds and other debt securities driven to historically low levels. These were just the latest in a series of bubbles stretching back through financial history. What causes bubbles? Why are the crashes that follow always so painful? Are they inevitably followed by recession? Who or what is to blame for the current crisis? And what can be done to prevent future bubbles?

Tulipmania (Holland): Tulips were first introduced to Europe from the Ottoman empire and by the early seventeenth century were highly prized in Holland. At the height of the boom in 1637, the highly sought-after Semper Augustus bulb was selling for 6,000 guilders - 20 times more than the cost of an average town house.

South Sea bubble (England): The South Sea Company was originally established to trade with South America. But in 1719, it did a deal with the British government to convert part of the national debt into company shares. The government benefited from a lower rate of interest, the company got a steady stream of interest income and investors swapped a dull bond for a racy share with growth prospects. The shares then soared in value from just over £120 in January 1720 to almost £1,000 by June of the same year, boosted by company bosses and politicians who had all been given free shares. By the end of the year, copycat companies were being listed on the stock exchange to cash in on the mania - one, famously, for a "venture whose purpose is yet to be decided" - before the market crashed and many were ruined.

Railway mania (England): The railway mania engulfed Britain in the 1840s, reaching its zenith in 1846 when Parliament passed 272 bills allowing new railway companies to be set up. The subsequent crash triggered the collapse of a number of banks and the granting of new powers to the Bank of England to act as lender of last resort to bail them out - a controversial move at the time. But the legacy of the boom was a much expanded rail network.

The Great Crash (US): In the 1920s, the US stock market soared on the back of explosive growth in demand for cars, radios, fridges and other household goods - which was in turn largely fuelled by the rise of widespread consumer credit. Between 1921 and its peak on September 3 1929, the Dow Jones Industrial Average, an index of the top 30 US stocks, rose six-fold. On Monday 28 October 1929 - known as Black Monday - the Dow suffered the largest one-day drop on record. By 1932, it had lost 90% of its value. In the subsequent Great Depression, US GDP shrank by a quarter.

Japanese bubble economy: Japan's post-war economic success left the country awash with savings, but with few outlets for ordinary people to invest abroad. The result was a spectacular bubble that in the 1980s infected every part of the economy. By 1989, the Nikkei index had risen 500% in a decade, while Japanese property prices had risen so far that it was said the emperor's palace in Tokyo was valued at more than the whole of California. The stock market eventually bottomed out in 2003 more than 80% below its peak, and Tokyo property prices are also still below their peak today.

Dotcom (US): Between 1995 and 2000, the US Nasdaq index of technology stocks rose five-fold, doubling in 1999 alone. The excitement centred on internet stocks - known as dotcoms. Few made any money or had many customers, yet once floated on the stock market they achieved sky-high valuations. In the subsequent crash, more than $5 trillion was wiped off technology stocks. The Nasdaq lost 80% of its value and even now only trades at around half of its peak.

Bubbles

In what way was the subprime debacle a bubble? It was actually the culmination of two bubbles. The first was a global credit bubble, in which the value of debt securities was driven to record highs, to the point where even the riskiest assets such as emerging market government bonds and junk bonds - bonds issued by highly indebted companies - were yielding little more than US government bonds, the safest bonds of all. In industry parlance, investors were completely mis-pricing risk. The second - related - bubble was in housing, notably in the US and UK, which fed off the availability of so much cheap debt.

Are bubbles an inevitable part of economic life? They seem to occur at frequent intervals in financial history. The Austrian economist J A Schumpeter writing in the 1930s saw bubbles as related to the business cycle, in which periods of over-investment were inevitably followed by a process of "creative destruction". But in the last few years, bubbles seem to be occurring more frequently, with bubbles in Japan, emerging markets, technology, US and UK housing - and, some now say, in commodities.

The third stage is euphoria, when the market becomes irrational...a phenomenon sometimes referred to as the "greater fool" theory of investing

Are all bubbles the same? No. But they do tend to have some features in common. The economist Charles Kindleberger, in his book Manias, Panics and Crashes identified three stages in the evolution of a bubble. The first is displacement - the emergence of a new discovery or technology that excites investor interest, such as the affordable motor car in the 1920s or the internet in the 1990s. The latest displacement was the growth in securitisation, which paved the way for a bubble in US housing.

The second phase is positive feedback: rising prices induce inexperienced investors to enter the market, such as subprime mortgage-holders and buy-to-let investors.

The third stage is euphoria, when the market becomes irrational. People buy assets simply because they believe they can sell them on later at a higher price - a phenomenon sometimes referred to as the "greater fool" theory of investing.

What conditions typically lead to a bubble? They tend to occur at times of social, political and economic stability. That means that people not only feel prosperous, but expect to continue to prosper. Invariably bubbles are accompanied by talk of a new era, which convinces people that the world is now operating according to a new set of rules. That is important, because it makes possible a huge expansion in credit, which is the hallmark of any bubble.

Why is credit so important to a bubble? Credit helps push asset prices far higher than they would otherwise go. The more confident people become that prices will continue rising, the more they will want to borrow. And the higher asset prices rise, the more banks are willing to lend. In the recent boom in US and UK housing, much of this credit took the form of mortgages. But during a bubble, an equally important source of credit expansion is the willingness of banks to lend "on margin".

What does "on margin" mean? It means that the bank puts up

part of the money to help the investor buy the asset. If the price of the asset goes up, the investor gets to pocket the profit. But if the price of the asset falls, the investor will be faced with a margin call - a demand to hand over money to cover the shortfall. Margin investing played a major part in the 1920s stock market bubble and again in the recent credit bubble when banks lent freely to hedge funds to buy credit securities. Some say it encourages speculation.

Speculators are usually said to be motivated purely by short-term gains

What is speculation? Speculation is much easier to identify in theory than to spot in practice. Speculators are usually said to be motivated purely by short-term gains. This marks them out from investors, who are interested in long-term returns. But that can often be a difficult distinction to make. At various times during the recent bubble, many groups could be accused of speculation, including hedge funds, private equity groups and buy-to-let investors, even though some of these might hold investments for years.

Is speculation bad? Not necessarily. Speculators can play a useful role in a market, providing a ready supply of buyers and sellers necessary to make a market. They are said to provide "liquidity" to the market. The snag is that in a crash, all that liquidity has a tendency to disappear.

Why does liquidity disappear in a crash?
Partly because everybody is trying to sell at once. But once the crash has started, the crisis is compounded by leveraged investors - those that have bought assets using borrowed money - selling assets to meet margin calls. That can create a vicious circle in which the further prices fall, the more people are forced to sell, leading to further falls in prices.

Has there been much forced selling in the current crisis? Yes. Many players were forced to start dumping US subprime mortgage securities early in the crisis because their funding dried up the moment prices started to fall. That wave of selling then triggered margin calls for other highly leveraged investors, most of whom are obliged to recalculate the value of their portfolios each day - a process known as "mark to market". The result is that investors may be forced to dump assets at fire sale prices - that is, whatever price they can get.

One of the features of a crash is that they tend to spread quickly to other assets

Have mortgage securities been dumped at fire sale prices?
It looks that way. Even the Bank of England in its May Financial Stability Review took the unusual step of stating that some mortgage securities had fallen too far, noting that prices of 2006 US subprime mortgage securities implied that 76% of borrowers would default on their mortgages and that banks would ultimately only recover 50% of the value of the properties.

No. One of the features of a crash is that they tend to spread quickly to other assets. That's because investors needing to liquidate assets to meet margin calls will often sell those that are easiest to sell - those for which there is still a liquid market - rather than sell a distressed asset at fire sale prices. In the early days of the credit crunch, this led to some big falls in share prices.

How can this vicious spiral be stopped? It will only stop when investors feel confident prices have stopped falling. That usually requires someone with deep pockets to step into the markets and start buying. In 1907, the legendary banker J.P. Morgan walked on to the floor of the New York Stock Exchange and started buying shares, thereby ending the so-called Bankers' Panic, when the market had fallen 50% from its peak.

More recently, the Federal Reserve - the US central bank - persuaded Wall Street banks to club together to buy up the assets of failed hedge fund Long Term Capital Management (LTCM) to halt the slide in the markets in 1989. In the current crisis, JP Morgan's rescue of Bear Stearns - with Fed assistance - seemed to halt the market slide.

Aftermath of crashes

Does a crash always lead to a recession? This is a topic of intense debate among economists. Some market crashes have been followed by deep recessions - although sometimes there is a time lag before the economic consequences become fully apparent. The South Sea bubble and Railway mania were both followed by economic crises. The Great Crash of 1929 was followed by the Great Depression in the 1930s. And the

Japanese market crash was followed by more than a decade of economic stagnation. On the other hand, the 1987 stock market crash was followed by two years of strong growth, as was the 1998 crisis following the collapse of LTCM. Meanwhile the bursting of the dotcom bubble led to only a very mild US recession and none at all in the UK.

The challenge is to prevent the crash affecting the real economy

What explains these different outcomes? The challenge is to prevent the crash affecting the real economy. In theory, there is no reason why it should, since the price of stocks and bonds should not make much difference to the underlying performance of the business. But in practice, crashes can affect the economy in two ways. Either the banks are hit by such large losses that they stop lending. Or consumers become so nervous at the declines in the markets that they stop spending - a phenomenon known as the wealth effect. Trying to avoid either of these outcomes is the task of policymakers, particularly central bankers.

Greenspan is widely held responsible for the current crisis for his decision to cut interest rates to 1% in 2002

What can policymakers do? Their task is to keep banks lending and consumers spending. Typically, the surest way to do this is to cut overnight interest rates, both to reduce the burden of existing debt and encourage people to borrow more. This was the policy pursued by Alan Greenspan, the former US Federal Reserve governor, in the aftermath of the 1987, 1998 and 2001 market crashes.

Was Greenspan successful? Greenspan was Fed chairman for 18 years. During that time, the US suffered only two periods of negative growth: in 1990-1 and a mild slowdown in 2001 in the wake of the dotcom crash and 9/11. But critics argue that his policy of slashing interest rates in response to the bursting of bubbles only fuelled future bubbles, both by encouraging reckless borrowing and by persuading the markets that the Fed would always ride to their rescue. Greenspan is widely held responsible for the current crisis for his decision to cut interest rates to 1% in 2002 - a move that fuelled the housing bubble.

Preventing bubbles

Why does no one intervene to prevent bubbles? Because they are much easier to spot with hindsight than they are at the time. Even at the height of bubbles, there will often be many who believe that prices are rational. In 1929, the eminent Yale economist Irving Fisher famously stated that shares had reached a "permanently high plateau", days before the Great Crash. Besides, policymakers do not feel it is their job to second-guess the market.

The Japanese experience in the 1990s had shown the dangers of falling retail prices

Could Greenspan have done more to prevent the current crisis?
Perhaps. It may be that Greenspan allowed US interest rates to remain too low for too long. But at the time, he was more concerned with preventing deflation, which appeared a genuine risk. The Japanese experience in the 1990s had shown the dangers of falling retail prices, with consumers refusing to spend and banks refusing to lend, even though interest rates were cut to 0%.

What can be done to prevent future bubbles? One option is to require central banks to pay more attention to asset prices when setting interest rates. At the moment, most focus only on retail price inflation, which until very recently had been very low worldwide for many years - largely as a result of globalisation and the impact of new technology. That meant interest rates remained low even as asset prices soared.

Is more regulation the answer? All bubbles are followed by new regulation - and new rules for the banking industry are already under discussion as a result of the current crisis. But there is always a balance to be struck to ensure that draconian new rules do not end up stamping out healthy risk-taking, creativity and innovation.

The recent credit bubble has left its mark in the form of the regeneration of many British towns and cities

Does any good come out of bubbles? Yes. Bubbles may be associated with irrational exuberance, but they invariably leave a legacy of new infrastructure. Past bubbles have brought the world canals, railways, roads and the internet. The recent credit bubble has left its mark in the form of the regeneration of many British towns and cities, while globally it helped lift millions out of poverty.

Bubbles – the issues

Bubbles are a regular feature of economic life. They are usually identified with a new technology or invention and often occur at times of social stability and political optimism.

As with all bubbles, the current crisis was the result of excessive credit, which meant many investors were forced to dump assets at fire sale prices when values started to fall.

Market crashes are often followed by a recession – but not always. Much depends on how successfully policymakers can prevent the impact of the crash seeping into the real economy.

The US has generally recovered well from crashes in the last 20 years, largely due to former Fed chairman Alan Greenspan's willingness to slash interest rates.

Many economists blame Greenspan for the current crisis, arguing that he cut interest rates too low following the dotcom bust, thereby sowing the seeds for the housing and credit bubbles.

Crashes always bring demands for fresh regulation, but these need to be balanced against the risk of stifling risk-taking, creativity and innovation.

Although market crashes are painful at the time, bubbles usually leave a lasting legacy in the form of new infrastructure. The recent bubble helped lift two million people out of poverty.

Bank runs

The enduring image of the credit crunch is that of people queuing outside Northern Rock branches in September 2007 as they tried to get their money out of the stricken lender. It was the first run on a UK bank in 140 years and led to Northern Rock being nationalised five months later. In March 2008, a similar crisis of confidence led to the collapse of US investment bank Bear Stearns which was rescued over a weekend by JP Morgan. Why are banks treated differently to other businesses? Why are some considered too big to fail? And what can be done to prevent future bank failures?

What causes a run on a bank? A sudden loss of confidence in the bank. All banks make their money primarily by borrowing money cheaply on a short-term basis from depositors, other banks and the credit markets and lending it long-term at a higher rate in the form of mortgages and other types of long-term lending. For this to work, all banks need to keep enough ready cash to hand to ensure that all depositors and lenders to get their money out immediately if they want to. The problems arise if too many people want to get their money out and the bank can't find the cash.

Northern Rock

Is this what happened at Northern Rock? Yes. The initial problem arose in August 2007 when the wholesale money markets used by the Newcastle-based bank to fund about 80% of its mortgage lending effectively closed up. Northern Rock needed to refinance up to £4bn of its borrowings by the end of October. Without access to fresh finance, it risked defaulting on its debt.

Northern Rock accounted for one in every five new mortgages

Why would no one lend to Northern Rock? Because no one trusted the quality of its mortgage book. It had been one of the most aggressive lenders during the UK housing market bubble and was notorious for its "Together" mortgages, which enabled first-time buyers to borrow up to 125% of the value of their home. In the first half of 2007, it accounted for one in every five new mortgages in the country and was the fastest growing bank in Britain. But this growth was achieved at the expense of a growing reliance on the money markets.

How did Northern Rock resolve the situation? By the 14th September 2007, it had become clear that Northern Rock was not going to find new funding in the markets. The Bank of England tried to engineer a rescue bid by Lloyds TSB, a much larger and more solid bank. But these talks came to nothing.

Why was there no rescue from Lloyds? Accounts differ. It's not clear how serious the offer was, but it was dependent on a substantial taxpayer loan that the government did not want to provide. There may have been legal obstacles to pushing through a deal, which would have taken weeks to complete. But these may be excuses. At the time, no one knew how serious the financial crisis was to become. If they had, it seems likely they would have found a way to force Northern Rock into the arms of a buyer.

So what happened to Northern Rock? It was forced to ask the Bank of England for emergency funding in its capacity as lender of last resort to the UK banking system. The news broke that evening, causing alarm amongst Northern Rock savers, many of whom tried to get their money out of their accounts via the internet that night. When the website crashed, they queued outside the branches the next morning. The run on the bank continued over the weekend until the government was forced to issue a statement guaranteeing all deposits.

How much did the Bank of England lend Northern Rock? The Bank of England is thought to have initially lent Northern Rock £2bn, but this rose rapidly over the following days and weeks as depositors withdrew their savings. By the end of 2007, Northern Rock was reckoned to owe the Bank £28bn. And by the time it was nationalised in February, the government was on the hook for £55bn.

By the time Northern Rock was nationalised, the government was on the hook for £55bn

By the time Northern Rock was nationalised, the government was on the hook for £55bn

Rescuing banks

Are bank runs common? No. Before Northern Rock, the last run on a UK retail bank was in 1866 with the collapse of Overend, Guerney & Co. Since then, there have been a number of other banking crises, most notably the 1974 secondary banking crisis, when a number of fringe banks collapsed as a result of the downturn in the UK property market. The last significant UK bank failure prior to Northern Rock was the collapse of Barings in 1994 as a result of a giant fraud by rogue trader Nick Leeson.

What happened to Barings? Leeson had built up a large, unauthorised, loss-making position betting on a rise in the Japanese stock market. That position suddenly deteriorated as a result of the Kobe earthquake. As word of Barings' huge position got out, the rest of the market started betting against it. Soon the paper loss was more than £800m - more than enough to wipe out Barings capital. The Bank of England refused to step in to help, but the Dutch Bank ING agreed to take over Barings and its debts for £1.

Some banks have always been considered "too big to fail"

Why was Northern Rock rescued? In theory, a bank should be no different to any other private business: if it gets into trouble as a result of its own bad lending practices, then its shareholders and customers should suffer the consequences. In practice, however, some banks have always been considered "too big to fail" and the central bank and government steps in to bail them out.

Why are some banks "too big to fail"? Because of the fears of "systemic risk" - that their collapse will in turn trigger the collapse of other banks, at which point the supply of credit to the economy will dry up causing massive financial distress. This was what happened in the 1930s in America, leading to the Great Depression. There is no hard rule as to what constitutes "too big to fail". Northern Rock was only a medium-sized bank, but the authorities decided to bail it out in case its collapse led to a loss of confidence in other smaller banks such as Alliance & Leicester and Bradford & Bingley.

Bank regulation - and deregulation

Can any bank apply for emergency funding? No. Only those banks with accounts with the central bank can access lender of last resort facilities, which usually means only retail deposit taking banks. Since public money is at stake, they have to accept in return for this privilege strict rules regarding the way they conduct their business, including holding an agreed amount of money in cash or government securities at the Bank and limits on the amount of capital they must hold for a given level of lending.

Is this the way it works in the US too? In the US, only commercial banks have accounts with the US Fed. These are banks like Citigroup that take retail deposits and whose business is primarily that of making loans. They are different to investment banks - sometimes known as broker-dealers - which are engaged in issuing and trading securities. In theory, this means that investment banks such as Goldman Sachs and Lehman Brothers cannot be bailed out by the Fed.

Investment banks such as Goldman Sachs and Lehman Brothers cannot be bailed out by the Fed

Why does the Fed make this distinction? It is largely a hangover from history. In response to the collapse of the US banking system in the 1930s, the US government passed the Glass Steagal Act that forced banks to become either commercial or investment banks. That led to the enforced break-up of some the biggest names on Wall Street such as JP Morgan. This legislation was designed to keep lending banks out of the securities business, where it was believed they would inevitably use their balance sheets to lend to investors, thereby fueling future bubbles. But this distinction between commercial and investment banks has now become blurred, particularly since the Glass Steagal Act was repealed in 1994.

Why was Glass Steagal repealed? Largely because it was becoming increasingly hard to police. The growth of the securitisation markets - in particular the mortgage securitisation market - was blurring the distinction between the loan business and securities. In addition, bankers and regulators thought they had discovered better ways to measure and manage risk that paved the way for less onerous - but supposedly more effective - bank regulation that focused on setting out detailed rules on the amount of capital they had to hold for different types of risk.

The first US bank to collapse in the credit crunch was Bear Stearns, an investment bank

Was it a mistake to repeal Glass Steagal? Some people blame the repeal of Glass Steagal - along with a number of other moves to deregulate banking in the 1980s and 1990s - for the fuelling of the credit bubble. What is not up for debate is that its repeal paved the way for a wave of bank mergers and an explosion in the securitisation and the even more racy structured credit markets, which used derivatives to allow investors to gain huge exposures to the securities markets using borrowed money. Perhaps not surprisingly, the first US bank to collapse in the credit crunch was Bear Stearns, an investment bank.

Bear Stearns

Why did Bear Stearns collapse? Bear was an early victim of the credit crunch when two in-house hedge funds defaulted on their debts, forcing the bank to pump $3.2bn into one fund to rescue it while the other was left to collapse. Bear Stearns was also a major player in the credit derivatives market and was one of the biggest lenders to hedge funds through its prime broking business. Bear's problem was that, like Northern Rock, it relied on the markets for its own funding. As the credit crisis dragged on, investors started to worry about whether Bear would be able to continue to fund itself. Those fears became self-fulfilling when Bear's customers, particularly the hedge funds, started to panic and withdrew their funds, just as they had at Northern Rock.

How did the Fed respond? As a broker-dealer, Bear Stearns did not have an account at the Fed. But the Fed quickly decided Bear was too big to fail. As a counterparty to hundreds of billions of dollars of credit derivatives, the consequences of it being allowed to collapse could have brought down the global financial system. Confidence in other broker dealers, such as Lehman Brothers, would have vanished. The Fed would have been confronted by a string of banking collapses. The Fed's response was therefore to provide JP Morgan, a much larger bank, with a $30bn facility that it could pass straight on to Bear. That kept Bear alive until the weekend, when a deal for JP Morgan to takeover Bear was hammered out.

The Fed was concerned to make sure that Bear shareholders were punished for the bank's failure

Was this deal fair to Bear's shareholders? Bear Stearns shareholders were initially offered just $2 per share - a fraction of what they had been worth a year before when they traded at $150 a share, and well below their closing price on the day before the Fed rescue, when they had traded at $30 per share. This was later upped to $10 a share. But the takeover terms reflected the fact that Bear was effectively bankrupt and the takeover could only go ahead because the Fed was willing to provide public money to protect JP Morgan from the risks. More importantly, the Fed was concerned to make sure that Bear shareholders were punished for the bank's failure to guard against moral hazard.

What is meant by moral hazard? Moral hazard is the risk that bailing out reckless behaviour by financial institutions will only encourage further reckless behaviour in the future. In the case of Northern Rock and Bear Stearns, central banks attempted to minimise moral hazard by ensuring that senior executives lost their jobs and that shareholders received minimal value for their shares in the subsequent takeover.

Will there be more bank failures in this crisis? Quite possibly. But the willingness of the Fed and Bank of England to step in over Bear Stearns and Northern Rock makes it unlikely that the collapse of any other bank during this crisis will lead to a systemic crisis - in other words a domino effect leading to the collapse of other banks. Any future runs on banks are likely to be result of individual bank losses giving rise to doubts about its solvency.

What can be done to stop future bank runs? The collapse of Northern Rock has already led to moves to strengthen the UK government's guarantee to protect bank retail deposits. That should reduce the likelihood of future scenes of depositors queuing round the block to get their money out. Regulators are also working on tightening up the rules concerning bank capital requirements and also ensuring they have more diverse and longer-term sources of funding so they are not so vulnerable if one market seizes up.

Bank runs - the issues

Bank runs are caused by a sudden loss of confidence in a bank, leading to customers all trying to withdraw their money at once.

Until the collapse of Northern Rock, the last run on a UK bank was the collapse of Overend, Guerney in 1866.

Northern Rock collapsed because it was unable to secure new funding in the wholesale money markets and was forced to turn to the Bank of England for an emergency loan.

Banks are not like other private businesses; some are considered "too big to fail" because of the risk their collapse might lead to a run on other banks and the collapse of the financial system.

Northern Rock was deemed too big to fail because of the risk its collapse might lead to problems for other UK mortgage banks.

JP Morgan ultimately rescued Bear Stearns with the backing of the US Fed for similar reasons; its collapse threatened a systemic banking crisis.

Bear Stearns shareholders ultimately received minimal compensation for their shares to guard against the risk of moral hazard.

Ending the credit crunch

The problem with a financial crisis is that it can quickly develop a momentum of its own, spreading to other markets far removed from the original source of trouble. And the longer it continues, the more likely it is that the crisis will infect the real economy, leading to job losses, business failures, recession - and even depression. In Britain, the credit crunch has already led to falling house prices and slower economic growth. But once a crisis has started, what can be done to stop it? And by who?

What will end the credit crunch? The vital ingredient is confidence. A financial system built on credit cannot operate without confidence. Banks need to be confident that their customers won't all demand their money back at the same time, causing a run on the bank. And they need to be confident that any money they lend they will get back. Otherwise they will hoard cash and refuse to lend, causing the system to grind to a halt.

Since August 2007, Libor has traded as much as 0.7 percentage points over base rates - an unprecedented spread

How can confidence be restored? The key is to restore the health of the banking system. One of the biggest problems during the credit crunch has been the reluctance of the banks to lend to one another. The London Interbank Offered Rate (LIBOR) - the rate of interest banks charge each other to borrow - usually tracks closely the Bank of England base rate. But since August 2007, Libor has traded as much as 0.7 percentage points over base rates - an unprecedented spread.

Why were banks not lending to one another? Partly because they felt they needed to hoard cash to reassure their own customers; but it was also because they did not trust one another. They feared other banks might be sitting on large hidden losses or might be exposed to future losses if house prices - and other asset prices - kept falling.

How can banks be restored to health? In an ideal world, banks would sort out their own problems, just as failing businesses would be expected to do in any other industry. But banks aren't like other industries. So in practice, banks look to the authorities - the government and central banks - to help them out. The challenge in tackling a financial crisis is striking the right balance between how much the authorities should do to help, and how much the banks should be made to do for themselves.

The banks

What can the banks do to tackle the crisis? The most important thing they can do is to come clean about their losses - and, if necessary, raise enough new capital to reassure the market that they are still in good financial health. In the early stages of the credit crunch, one of the biggest problems was that the banks were slow to admit the scale of their exposure to risky assets.

Why were the banks slow to come clean? Largely because the banks did not believe the losses were for real. They assumed the initial slump in the market price of mortgage securities and leveraged loans was an over-reaction - the result of forced selling by hedge funds - and unlikely to be a real indication of what they might be worth. Most banks thought that if they held on for a few months, prices would bounce back.

The biggest losers were Citigroup, which wrote off $16.4bn

When did the banks start to admit their losses? The first big write-downs came in October and November 2007, when the major US banks and a few European banks were obliged to report third quarter results. The biggest losers were Citigroup, which wrote off $16.4bn, Merrill Lynch, which wrote off $7.9bn and UBS, which wrote off $4bn. Faced with these losses, many banks raised fresh capital to plug the holes in their balance sheets.

Where did they raise the capital? Much of it came from so-called sovereign wealth funds - the hugely powerful investment arms of the governments of various Middle Eastern and Asian countries. Between them, these state-run funds control some $2.9 trillion of assets. Sovereign wealth funds took significant stakes in many of the big US investment banks, including Citigroup, Merrill Lynch and Morgan Stanley as well as several European banks such as UBS, Credit Suisse and Barclays in the UK. The banks hoped that by coming clean about their losses and raising all this fresh capital, confidence would return.

Did all this do the trick? No. The problem was that the banks had not marked down all their dodgy assets to market prices, believing those prices to be unrealistic. Yet the prices of those assets continued to fall, as the US housing slump got worse and more owners of those assets, such as hedge funds, started dumping them on the market at firesale prices. By the end of the first quarter of 2007, the banks were forced to make a further round of giant write-downs and some had to raise even more capital.

How much did they write off this time? The biggest casualty was the Swiss bank UBS, which had by now written off a total $37bn and was forced to raise $15bn by selling new shares. But all the big global banks were hit, including many of the UK banks, which had only reported small losses at the end of 2007. Royal

Bank of Scotland reported losses of £6bn and raised £12bn of fresh equity. The difference was that this time, the banks marked down the value of their problem mortgage bonds closer to market values. By the end of May 2008, the total losses from the credit crunch had hit $386bn.

By the end of May 2008, the total losses from the credit crunch had hit $386bn

Was this enough to restore confidence in banks? In the short-term at least, yes. Fears of a systemic crisis - multiple bank failures leading to the collapse of the financial system - had begun to recede, although credit conditions still remained tight, creating problems in the real economy. In April 2008, the rate at which banks could borrow from each other started to come down closer to official bank rates. But this shift in the outlook also owed much to assistance from central banks.

Policymakers

What can central banks do to help? They have two basic weapons at their disposal. The first is to cut overnight interest rates in the hope that cheaper borrowing costs will keep the economy going. The second is to pump money into the banking system to ensure the banks have enough cash to keep functioning. The purpose of these so-called liquidity operations is to ensure banks don't go bust because they have run out of money.

Have central banks been cutting interest rates? The US cut interest rates from 5.25% to 2% by the end of May 2008. The UK has been slower to cut rates, so far bringing them down by only three quarters of a percentage point to 5%. All the central banks have also pumped significant extra cash into the financial system.

The Bank of England is worried about inflation, which has been rising, largely as a result of higher food and fuel prices

Why has the Bank of England not cut rates as fast as the Fed? Because the Bank is worried about inflation, which has been rising, largely as a result of higher food and fuel prices. Inflation is currently higher than the Bank's target of 2%. Inflation is also rising in the US, but the Fed has a more flexible mandate that includes maintaining growth as well as controlling inflation. It has no specific inflation target.

How effective have rate cuts been? Not as effective as central banks might have hoped. One problem is that lenders are not passing on rate cuts to their customers. Rate cuts can only ease the pressure on borrowers if borrowers can get access to cheaper credit. In the UK, banks have actually raised mortgage rates despite the rate cuts and many cheap mortgage deals have been withdrawn.

Why have banks put up mortgage rates? Because their own borrowing costs are rising as a result of the squeeze in the interbank market. The closure of the securitisation markets means there is a lot less money available to fund new lending - banks cannot sell on loans but must fund any new lending from their own balance sheet. The result is that demand for money exceeds supply, pushing up its price.

Demand for money exceeds supply, pushing up its price

What can central banks do to ease the supply? They can pump more money into the banking system. The way they do this is to increase the amount of money they allow banks to borrow from them. The snag is that to borrow from central banks, the banks must deposit with them ultra-high quality collateral, such as government bonds, that the central bank can keep if the bank is unable to repay. During the credit crunch, many banks found they did not have enough government bonds to deposit to raise the amount of cash they needed.

Why did they find themselves in this position? Because large parts of the credit markets had effectively closed. For example, many banks had large portfolios of mortgage securities that they used to raise short-term cash via the so-called repo market - in normal times, a highly liquid market widely used by all financial institutions. But as the subprime crisis unfolded, the prices of these mortgage securities plummeted to the point where the repo market would no longer lend against them. That left the banks with a huge gap in their funding.

How did central banks respond? By widening the range of collateral they would accept to include some mortgage securities.

The European Central Bank did this almost immediately in August 2007, while the Fed relaxed its lending conditions in stages, with a series of new initiatives to ease bank funding problems. The Bank of England was the most cautious, initially only making small amounts of money available for borrowing against mortgage securities and only for short periods. However, in April 2008, it changed tack and made at least £50bn available to banks for up to three years.

Why was the Bank of England so slow to act? Because it did not want to be seen to be bailing out the banks at the first sign of trouble. That would have set a very bad precedent and encouraged future reckless lending. The Bank was also anxious not to do anything that would have exposed taxpayers to potential losses.

Are taxpayers now exposed to losses? The Bank of England's £50bn scheme was carefully designed to minimise the risks to taxpayers. The Bank said it would only accept the highest quality mortgage securities. It also set strict limits on the amount it would lend for every £1 of collateral - known in the financial world as a "haircut". And it insisted that if any mortgage securities fell in value, the banks would have to replace them. The Bank would only be exposed to losses if a bank became insolvent.

Have these central bank operations done the trick? They certainly make the risk that another bank goes bust because it can't access funding - which is what happened to Northern Rock and Bear Stearns - much less likely. But these operations can't protect the bank against the credit risks - the risk that past poor lending decisions will lead to future losses. Nor does the extra funding mean the banks will start lending as freely as they did before.

If all else fails, governments and central banks can always step in

What if the crisis continues? There are still other things the central banks can do. They can continue to relax their collateral requirements to accept more risky mortgage securities. And they can loosen their terms to the point where the bank is taking on more of the credit risk from dodgy assets. And if all else fails, governments and central banks can always step in to the market to buy dodgy mortgage securities outright. That is what the US government ultimately did in the 1930s.

Ending the credit crunch – the issues

For the credit crunch to end, confidence must return to the banking system. Until then, banks will continue to be reluctant to lend to one another and borrowing costs will remain high.

In the early stages of the crisis, banks were slow to come clean about the scale of their losses or to raise new capital. That made other banks nervous about lending to each other.

Central banks have two main weapons available in a crisis: they can cut interest rates to lower borrowing costs, and they can pump money into the financial system to ease funding pressures.

The US Fed has cut interest rates aggressively during the credit crunch, but European central banks have been slower because of fears of rising inflation.

Central banks pumped hundreds of billions of dollars of cash into the banking system during the crisis because many of the markets that banks usually use to borrow money were closed.

In theory, these operations expose taxpayers to credit risks - although in practice the terms have been set to minimise these risks.

In an extreme crisis, central banks can take on more of the credit risk - or the government can even buy the dodgy assets outright, as happened in the 1930s.

The key players

The public bodies and organisations
involved with our money

Who are the people at the heart of the credit crunch? From governments trying to tackle the problem to hedge fund managers and private equity firms, Pocket Issue rounds up those who are in the eye of the storm.

Policymakers

Who is leading the global response to the credit crunch? Central banks. Their functions vary from country to country, but generally, they operate on behalf of governments to set overnight interest rates, issue currency, act as banker to the government, oversee the stability of the financial system and act as lender of last resort to the banking system. In the US, the central bank is the **Federal Reserve**; in the EU, the **European Central Bank** (ECB); and in the UK, the **Bank of England.**

What tools do central banks have to fight the credit crunch? They have two main tools. The first is monetary policy - the ability to set interest rates. This should lower the cost of servicing existing debts. The second is so-called open market operations - the ability to pump money into the financial system by increasing the amount of cash the central bank is willing to lend to other banks. In a crisis, the central bank can also act as lender of last resort to a troubled bank, making sure it has access to enough cash to meet its obligations by assuming its liabilities.

Who runs the US Federal Reserve? **Ben Bernanke** has been chairman of the US Fed since 2006, when he took over from **Alan Greenspan.** An academic by training, Bernanke had made his name as an expert on the Great Depression. Later, as a member of the Fed board under Greenspan, Bernanke acquired the nickname "Helicopter Ben" after stating he would throw dollar bills out of a helicopter if that was what it took to stop the US sliding into deflation. Critics took that to mean he would be reckless with inflation.

What has been his response to the crisis so far? Bernanke has already cut interest rates aggressively from 5.5% to 2%. He has also pumped huge amounts of extra cash into the financial system through emergency loans to banks, and he has widened the collateral the Fed is willing to accept for those loans to include mortgage securities, as well as government bonds.

How successful has he been? Bernanke won plaudits for his handling of the collapse of Bear Stearns, helping to engineer a takeover by JP Morgan over the weekend, with the help of a $30bn Fed guarantee. That swift action almost certainly prevented a major systemic crisis that could have seen several other major banks collapse. But Bernanke has also been criticised for taking risks with inflation by cutting interest rates too far.

The UK

Who runs the Bank of England? The current Governor is **Dr. Mervyn King**, who like Ben Bernanke started his career as an academic, before becoming chief economist at the Bank. He has a reputation as a "hawk" who is particularly vigilant on inflation risks and alert to the dangers of moral hazard if central banks are too willing to bail out reckless banks.

How has King responded to the crisis? So far, the Bank's Monetary Policy Committee (MPC) has cut interest rates by 0.75 percentage points - far less than the US Fed - reflecting the

MPC's concern over rising inflation. The US Fed must take economic growth as well as inflation into account when setting interest rates, but the Bank only has one goal: to hit the government's 2% inflation target. The Bank was also slow to pump money into the UK banking system after the crisis broke in August and was slower than other central banks to widen the collateral it was prepared to accept in return for loans.

How successful has King been? King has attracted criticism from the City and Whitehall, both of which would have liked him to have acted sooner to provide emergency support to the banks. He has also been criticised for failing to secure a quick solution to the problems at Northern Rock. But King's supporters say that his job is to protect taxpayers, not come to the rescue of irresponsible banks at the first sign of trouble. Besides, some mistakes should be blamed on problems in the UK regulatory structure.

What is wrong with the UK regulatory structure? Unlike most other central banks, the Bank of England is no longer responsible for supervising individual banks. It was stripped of this important function in 1997 and the powers handed to the Financial Services Authority (FSA). As a result, the UK now has a "tripartite" system of financial regulation in which the Treasury, the Bank and the FSA are jointly responsible for tackling a crisis. Northern Rock exposed serious flaws in this system. It wasn't clear who was in charge; the Bank didn't have adequate powers to intervene; and the Bank's lack of contact with other banks may have meant it was slow to appreciate the scale of the crisis.

Will the system be reformed? The government has promised an overhaul of the tripartite regime. The Bank will not be given back responsibility for supervising banks but it will be put in charge of a Special Resolution Regime with new powers to intervene in failing banks.

Who runs the European Central Bank? The current chairman is **Jean-Claude Trichet**, the former head of the Banque de France. He is also seen as an inflation hawk.

How has Trichet responded to the credit crunch? The ECB was the first to pump emergency funding into the financial system when the crisis broke in August 2007. However, the ECB has so far not cut interest rates, leaving them at 4%, due to concern about the euro zone's persistent high inflation. Indeed, Trichet has even suggested he will raise rates if inflation remains high. These high interest rates have caused problems for those euro zone countries, such as Spain and Ireland, which have been most caught up in the credit crunch.

Governments

What can governments do to ease the credit crunch? Governments only have limited tools to tackle the credit crunch since most have handed control of monetary policy to independent central banks. That means government action is confined for the most part to fiscal policy - taxing and spending. Modern economic orthodoxy - as set out by the British economist John Maynard Keynes in response to the Great Depression - is that governments should respond to a slump by cutting taxes and increasing spending.

Have governments been doing this? The US government has increased borrowing substantially, not least to fund a tax cut for every taxpayer in America. However, the UK government has not been able to cut taxes or raise spending significantly because borrowing is already close to the government's self-imposed ceiling of 40% of GDP.

Could governments do more? If the crisis gets really serious, there is plenty more governments can do, from relaxing the central bank's inflation target, providing direct support to homeowners or the mortgage market and assuming some of the banks' credit risk. The one constraint is a government's credibility in the bond markets. If international investors lose faith, it could lead to a collapse of the currency and higher interest rates to finance the national debt, making the economic crisis worse.

The Banks

Which banks have been most affected by the credit crisis? Between them, banks had written off more than $380bn by the end of May 2008, with the losses spread around the world. Apart from those banks that have already collapsed, such as Bear Stearns and Northern Rock, the worst affected are giant investment banks such as Citigroup, Merrill Lynch and UBS.

Is the worst over for the banks? Not necessarily. The International Monetary Fund estimates that total losses from the subprime crisis could total $1 trillion. Much depends on what happens to the US housing market. If it continues to slide, then further losses are inevitable. The longer the crisis continues, the more likely it will spread to other parts of the economy, leading to further losses on other types of debt such as corporate loans, student debt, credit cards and car loans.

How have the banks responded to the crisis? They have tried to build up their capital position to absorb any future losses. They have done this by curtailing their lending, cutting their dividends and raising fresh capital from investors such as sovereign wealth funds.

How have the UK banks performed? Most of the UK banks had some exposure to US subprime mortgages. Royal Bank of Scotland and Barclays in particular also had significant exposure to private equity leveraged loans. But the bigger worry is the banks' exposure to the UK housing market, which is now slowing rapidly.

Hedge funds

What is a hedge fund? A hedge fund is a private investment fund, typically only available to professional investors and the very rich, with the freedom to employ complex trading strategies such as short selling and using debt to juice up returns. Hedge funds grew in popularity during the 2001-2003 bear market, when they offered a way to make money in a falling stock market. There are now around 11,000 hedge funds in the world, controlling between them around $2.5 trillion of assets. London is the second biggest centre for hedge funds after New York.

How have they been affected by the credit crunch? Not as badly as feared. Before the crisis, hedge funds were seen as the main source of instability in the financial system. In fact, only a small number of hedge funds have collapsed - mostly those investing in credit securities. These include two funds run by Bear Stearns, which imploded early in the crisis. The most spectacular European hedge fund failure was Peloton, a $2bn London-based credit fund which collapsed in February 2008 due to excessive leverage. Meanwhile, some hedge funds have actually done well from the crisis.

How have hedge funds done well from the crisis? A few hedge fund managers bet on the US housing market crash by short selling mortgage securities, generating huge profits. US hedge fund manager John Paulson is reported to have personally made more than $3bn from this trade in 2007. Since the crisis started, other hedge funds have also made money from shorting banks and other financial stocks. However, this has proved controversial as some hedge funds have been accused of spreading rumours about banks such as HBOS in the UK and Lehman Brothers in the US, to drive down their share price.

Private equity

What is private equity? Private equity groups buy under-performing or fast-growing companies with the aim of improving their performance and selling them a few years later at a profit. Private equity will typically use large amounts of borrowed money to fund their acquisitions – a bit like using a mortgage to buy a house. During the credit bubble, the easy availability of debt on generous terms allowed private equity to go after ever-larger targets, including FTSE 100 firms such as Boots and J. Sainsbury.

Why was it able to raise money so easily? Because loans made to private equity firms were subject to the same slicing and dicing that made possible the huge explosion in the availability of mortgages. Banks packaged loans together and sliced them up and sold them to hedge funds and other investors, which left them free to make more loans. As banks became increasingly desperate to compete for private equity business, the terms of loans got increasingly easy, with multiples of cash flow rising and important banking covenants being waived, leading to so-called covenant-lite loans.

What happened to the loan market in the credit crunch? When the credit crunch hit in August 2007, the loan market effectively closed overnight. At the time, banks had more than $300bn of loans on their balance sheets that they could no longer shift. That made it virtually impossible for the banks to write new loans, so buyout activity by the private equity groups stopped too. Many buyout loans are now trading at prices that suggest the market expects high levels of defaults. A year after the credit crunch started, banks are still sitting on nearly $200bn of loans.

What will happen to these loans? The banks are gradually trickling them out to the market, but often at big discounts to their par value - and in some cases the banks are having to offer further loans to the buyers to take them off their hands. But not all banks are willing to sell at current market prices since that would mean realising a loss. As long as the economy remains resilient, the banks hope the companies will keep up their interest payments, enabling them to recoup their money. But while these loans remain stuck on bank balance sheets, there is little prospect of future loans.

Rating agencies

What are rating agencies? Rating agencies analyse the creditworthiness of government and corporate bonds and other debt instruments, including mortgage-backed securities. This creditworthiness is expressed as a rating, with AAA being the highest - a gold standard awarded to only a handful of countries and very few companies. The three main rating agencies are Standard & Poors, Moody's and Fitch. During the boom, their ratings were widely relied upon by investors.

How reliable are their ratings? The agencies have a good track record with government and corporate bond ratings. The problem has been with structured finance, such as mortgage securities. Some of the more complex products rated AAA have been downgraded all the way to junk and some have suffered defaults. The credibility of the agencies has also been undermined by admissions of mistakes in their models. Even among those mortgage securities that have not been downgraded, prices have slumped as investor demand has evaporated. That has angered a lot of investors who argue that a AAA-rating should reflect liquidity as well as creditworthiness.

What will happen to ratings agencies? There are growing calls for greater regulation of ratings agencies. Many investors want the agencies to use a different scale to rate structured products, or adapt their ratings to reflect liquidity issues. In the meantime, investors are likely to rely less on ratings and do more of their own credit analysis.

Sovereign Wealth Funds

What is a sovereign wealth fund? Sovereign wealth funds are state-sponsored investment entities. One of the first sovereign funds was established by Norway in the 1950s to invest the proceeds of its North Sea oil. Sovereign funds are now common to many developing countries, particularly those with significant natural resource revenues, including most of the Gulf States. Between them, sovereign funds control more than $2 trillion.

How do they invest their money? Until recently, sovereign funds mostly invested in the bond markets. A few, such as the Abu Dhabi Investment Authority, invested in stock markets, but tended to take only small stakes in companies. Most preferred to keep a low profile and only a few were willing to take controlling stakes. But that has started to change, partly because the slide in the dollar and general weakness of the US economy has encouraged funds to seek alternatives to US bonds.

How have sovereign funds responded to the credit crunch? Sovereign funds came to the rescue of a number of banks early in the credit crunch by agreeing to buy stakes. For example, the government of Singapore bought a stake in UBS and the Chinese bought a stake in Barclays. Since then, bank shares have continued to slide which has embarrassed the sovereign funds and made them reluctant to put their hands in their pockets again. Nonetheless, they are sitting on top of huge piles of money and have an interest in repairing the global financial system. If the global outlook continues to worsen, sovereign funds could have a further role to play.

Stargazing

The good and the bad come 2010

zing

Boom or bust? Famine or feast? What will the impact of the credit
crunch be? Pocket Issue conjures up three possible scenarios
- one good, one bad, one terrible - come 2010.

Good outcome

By the end of 2008, the financial crisis is largely over.
Central banks pump enough money into the banking system to
prevent another Northern Rock or Bear Stearns-style bank run.
By allowing banks to deposit mortgage securities as collateral
for loans, central banks ensure no other bank is likely to go bust
as a result of lack of cash. That gives banks the confidence to
raise sufficient new capital to absorb losses from the slump in
the US and UK housing markets. Gradually, confidence returns to
the banking system, inter-bank borrowing rates fall, and prices of
financial assets start to rise as fears of further fire sales recede
and bargain-hunters start to appear.

Conditions in the real economy take longer to recover. UK house
prices continue to fall, which undermines consumer confidence
and makes life tough for retailers. But this is partly offset by
strong growth in exports as a result of a combination of the
weaker pound and booming demand from developing countries
such as China, Russia and India. The result is the UK only suffers
a mild downturn. Meanwhile, oil prices start to fall back from their
record highs as global demand for oil starts to fall. That leads
to lower inflation, paving the way for interest rate cuts in 2009.
As a result, the housing market gradually starts to pick up again.

Bad outcome

The financial crisis persists well into 2009. High oil prices feed through to higher inflation, which means central banks are forced to keep interest rates higher than they would like. As a result, house price falls in the US and UK prove worse than predicted, leading to further big losses that eat into bank capital. Reluctant to raise yet more capital on deeply unfavourable terms, the banks respond by restricting lending and raising the cost of borrowing. That feeds back into the real economy, leading to more personal and corporate defaults and a recession in the UK and US.

Ultimately, the recession proves short-lived. The oil price falls on the back of slowing demand, which brings down inflation and allows interest rates to be cut again. As borrowing costs fall, buyers start to return to the housing market and corporate profits pick up. Banks are able to write back some of their losses as they reverse, boosting their capital position and paving the way for more lending. By 2010, the economy is growing healthily again.

Doomsday outcome

The financial crisis goes from bad to worse. Central banks in a number of developing countries, including China, India and Russia, are forced to put up interest rates to contain runaway inflation that is threatening their domestic stability. Many emerging markets had kept interest rates low to maintain the value of their currencies against the dollar. The collapse of these currency pegs triggers a plunge in the dollar and sterling, leading to a sharp rise in inflation in the West. The Fed and the Bank of England are forced to respond with higher interest rates. The result is a major recession, with savage falls in house prices and big rises in personal bankruptcies, job losses and corporate defaults.

The recession adds to the pressures on the banking system. As the losses mount, doubts emerge about the solvency of many financial institutions, making it almost impossible to raise fresh capital. With no other banks willing to rescue struggling institutions, the US and UK governments are forced to step in, leading to a wave of Northern Rock-style nationalisations. They also try to ease the pressure on the banking system by agreeing to take on more of the credit risk from dodgy mortgages. That puts further pressure on government finances at a time when tax revenues are in freefall from the economic slowdown. The result is a loss of international investor confidence in the US and UK. Both countries are forced to hike interest rates again to finance their national debt, leading to yet more economic hardship. In 2010, there is still no end to this cycle in sight.

What can you do?

How you can make a mark

What can you do?

Managing your own finances during a credit crunch can be daunting. But there are some simple steps you can take to help you ride the storm and keep your bank balance in the black.

Batten down the hatches

Pay off debts. If the credit crunch continues, the cost of borrowing may rise even if interest rates are cut. Some forms of borrowing that people relied on during the boom may disappear altogether or become a lot harder to obtain, such as 0% balance transfer deals on credit cards. Where possible try to pay off your debts or lock in interest rates on your debts for the long-term.

Fix your mortgage. If you're one of the 1.4m people in Britain whose cheap mortgage deal is due to expire this year, you will need to act early to lock in a new deal. Cheap deals are becoming scarce and many disappear very quickly. People without much equity in their home may struggle to find a new lender willing to take them on, in which case prepare for a sharp rise in bills.

Build up your cash reserves. During times of economic uncertainty, it makes sense to build up your cash savings in case of emergencies. Fortunately, the interest payable on savings accounts has risen as a result of the credit crunch as banks are competing to build up deposits.

First step. Shop around for financial products that are the best fit for your needs: have a look at www.moneysupermarket.com for a comprehensive overview of what is available, and the terms and conditions on offer.

Investments – what should you choose?

Is my money safe in the bank? Further bank failures cannot be ruled out, although the actions taken by the Bank of England and other central banks since the crisis started makes them less likely. But in any event, the UK government guarantees the first £35,000 of bank deposits and has said it will raise this to £50,000 when new bank rules are brought in later in 2008. That should be enough to cover the overwhelming majority of savings in bank accounts.

Is the stock market good value? Stock markets were never caught up in the boom to the same extent as house prices and bond markets - partly because they had only just recovered from the dotcom boom and bust. As a result, share prices have not fallen heavily since the credit crunch, except in those sectors most exposed such as banks and retailers. In fact, on most historical measures, shares don't look too expensive. But that depends partly on what happens to company earnings. If the economy deteriorates, then earnings will fall and shares will fall too.

What about bonds? Bonds performed very well over the last decade or so. Inflation was falling, which meant that interest rates fell too. At the same time, the economy was growing, so defaults were at all-time lows, and the global search for yield pushed up bond prices. But the outlook for bonds is now less certain. Inflation is rising, which is bad for bonds because higher interest rates generally means lower bond prices. Meanwhile, the tougher economic environment is already leading to rising default rates.

Should I invest in emerging markets? Emerging markets have continued to boom despite the credit crunch. That's partly because a number of countries, including China and the Gulf states, peg their currencies to the dollar. This means that as the US has cut interest rates, they have loosened monetary policy too, fuelling the boom. Indeed, demand from these countries has prevented the West from slipping into outright recession. But economists are divided on how much longer emerging markets can remain immune to the economic downturn in the rest of the world. Meanwhile, emerging market shares look high on most measures.

Should I buy gold? Gold is traditionally considered a safe haven in an economic crisis. The gold price has soared since the credit crunch began, reaching an all-time high of $1000 an ounce - although when you take account of inflation that is still below the level it reached during the 1980s. The problem with gold is that it does not pay you a return like other investments, or even cash, so the main reason to buy it is if you think inflation is about take off and cash won't hold its value.

What about other commodities? Prices of almost all raw materials, whether precious metals like gold, silver and platinum, metals such as iron ore and copper, or so-called soft commodities such as wheat and rice, have soared in the last few years, largely on the back of growing demand from developing countries such as China and India. But prices have also been driven higher by speculators such as hedge funds, leading some analysts to conclude that there is now a bubble in commodities that could burst at any moment.

First step: Get clued up on investments. Visit www.fool.co.uk, a site devoted to everything financial with a good section on all types of investments, so whether you are just starting out or planning for retirement it's worth a look.

Financial problems

What if I get into financial difficulties? The important thing is to face up to your difficulties early before they spiral out of hand. Prioritise your debts. If you don't keep up your mortgage payments you can lose your house. If you can't afford to make your payments, or lose your job, you should talk to your lender as soon as possible.

What if I can't find a solution? Then you will have to consider an Individual Voluntary Agreement (IVA). An IVA is an agreement with your creditors to settle your debts by paying a reduced amount for a period of typically five years, after which the remainder of the debt is written off. Inevitably, applying for an IVA will affect your credit rating, making it harder for you to borrow in future. An IVA has to be prepared by a licensed insolvency practitioner who will present your proposal at a meeting of your creditors.

First Step: Get some professional help. Take advantage of free, confidential and independent advice on debts, benefits, housing and many other problems, from the Citizens Advice Bureau, which has 3,000 bureaus in a range of locations around the country ranging from GP surgeries to colleges and courts. Advice can be had in a face-to-face setting, via the telephone or you may even be able to have a visit in your home. Go to www.adviceguide.org.uk to find out more.

Further reading

The best places to keep up-to-date

Further Reading

Hopefully this Pocket Issue has given you a clearer idea
of the issues surrounding the credit crunch. You can keep
in touch with the latest on the subject through
our blog: http://blog.pocketissue.com.

However, since we aim to fit in your pocket rather than weigh
down your briefcase, we certainly don't claim to have the last
word on a subject. Want to know more? The following are a few
suggestions on where to look.

Keeping up to date

The Bank of England. The Bank sets interest rates to keep
inflation low, issues banknotes and works to maintain a stable
financial system. Log onto www.bankofengland.co.uk for the
current bank rate, the current inflation rate and the latest
statements from the Bank, as well as much more
financial information.

Financial Services Authority. This regulator of all providers of
financial services in the UK has a website that talks to both
customers and firms. It also runs courses on money-related
subjects, often aimed at the layperson rather than the
professional, www.fsa.gov.uk.

Reading around the subject

Devil Take the Hindmost, by Edward Chancellor (Macmillan), is a
history of financial speculation.

Manias, Panics and Crashes, by Charles Kindleberger (Wiley),
offers a good history of financial crises.

Lombard Street, by Walter Bagehot (Wiley), provides a good description of money markets.

Only Yesterday, by Frederick Lewis (Wiley), is a first hand account of American life in the 1920s, including the Great Depression, by a former editor of Harper's Magazine.

All too much?

Tulip Fever, by Deborah Moggach (Vintage) is one for the sun lounger - a novel set in 17th century Amsterdam, the plot centres on the high stakes and passions aroused by a prized tulip bulb.

The glossary

Jargon-free explanation

Jargon-free explanations for some key terms and organisations.

AAA-rating: The highest possible rating for a bond or debt security awarded by a rating agency. Triple-A signifies that the likelihood of default is close to zero.

Alt-A: An intermediate class of US mortgage debt standing between subprime and prime.

Asset-backed security: A bond that is created by securitising a particular asset such as a residential or commercial mortgage or credit card receivables.

Bank run: A sudden loss of confidence in a bank that leads to customers all trying to withdraw their money at once.

Bond: A debt security that typically pays a fixed annual rate of interest (coupon) and is repayable in full on a given date in the future.

Bubble: A period of financial excess leading to extreme over-valuation of one or more types of asset.

Central bank: The monetary authority for a country or currency area.

Collateral: Security pledged for a loan.

Collateralised Debt Obligation (CDO): A highly leveraged fund that packages up fixed income securities such as mortgage bonds and leveraged loans, financed by various tranches of debt securities.

CDO Squared: A CDO that invests in other CDO securities.

Commercial Paper (CP): Short-term bonds, usually with a term of less than a year, issued by banks and other financial institutions and typically bought by investors looking for a higher yielding alternative to cash.

Conduit: An off-balance sheet vehicle widely used by banks during the credit bubble.

Coupon: The interest payable on a bond.

Default: Failure to make due payment on a loan or bond, whether of interest or principal.

Dividend: The income paid to the owners of equity.

Equity: The basic capital that supports an enterprise.

Fire sale: The rapid sale of assets by a distressed seller.

Gearing: Usually refers to the level of borrowing by a company. Also known as leverage.

Hedge fund: An investment fund that employs complex trading strategies including the use of leverage, derivatives and short-selling that are off-limits to funds targeted at ordinary investors.

Investment bank: A bank that is principally engaged in the arranging, trading and underwriting of securities, as opposed to a commercial bank, which is principally engaged in lending.

Jingle mail: A slang term that became popular after the bursting of the US housing bubble, and refers to the practice of homeowners unable to keep up payments on their mortgages sending the keys to their homes back to the bank by post.

Lender of last resort: In the event of a bank run, a central bank may step in to provide emergency funding to prevent it going bust.

Leverage: See gearing.

Leveraged buyout: A private equity bid for a business that relies on a small amount of equity and a large amount of debt.

Leveraged loan: Loans made to private equity firms during the boom to help fund leveraged buyouts.

Libor: The rate of interest at which banks will lend to one another.

Liquidity: The ease with which one can buy or sell a particular asset.

Margin and Margin Call: The amount of money an investor must deposit with a broker if they borrow to buy a stock. If the price of the stock falls, the broker will ask them to put up more cash, a demand known as a margin call.

Mark-to-market: The process by which banks and hedge funds are obliged to revalue their assets to reflect market prices.

Monetary policy: The setting of interest rates by a central bank.

Moral hazard: The risk that bailing out investors will only encourage even more reckless behaviour.

Off-balance sheet vehicle: An entity designed in such a way that its assets and liabilities do not appear on the sponsoring company's balance sheet.

Private equity: Equity investments that are not listed on a public stock market.

Rating agency: An organisation that provides fixed income - bonds and other debt securities - investors with credit analysis. The analysis is accompanied by a rating that signifies the rating agencies assessment of the creditworthiness of a security, with Triple-A being the highest.

Repo market: A market that allows banks and other financial institutions to borrow from one another short-term against a wide range of fixed income collateral.

Securitisation: The process whereby a stream of future income such as mortgage payments are turned into debt securities such as mortgage bonds.

Structured credit: A generic term referring to the whole range of complex debt securities that proliferated during the boom.

Structured investment vehicle (SIV): Like conduits, a type of off-balance sheet vehicle popular with banks and hedge funds that used commercial paper to fund large portfolios of mortgage bonds and other asset-backed securities.

Systemic crisis: A collapse in confidence affecting the whole financial system, leading to multiple bank failures. The US Federal Reserve feared the collapse of Bear Stearns would lead to a systemic crisis, which is why it stepped in to support a rescue by JP Morgan.

Subprime mortgage: Mortgages provided to homebuyers with poor credit records, whether because of previous credit problems or low and irregular income.

Tranche: A portion of a securitisation or structured credit after it has been sliced and diced to achieve a particular credit rating.

Write-down: The loss reported by a bank to reflect the value of assets it holds after they have been marked down to reflect market prices.

Yield and Dividend Yield: The income receivable from a security expressed as a proportion of its current market price. The yield on an equity is known as the dividend yield.

Notes

Some space for your notes...

Fat: eating ourselves to death?

July 2008

Rising obesity is causing life expectancy to fall for the first time in centuries, costing the NHS £3.7 billion a year. So why we are fatter as a nation than we have ever been before? Is obesity a choice or an illness? And why is childhood obesity at epidemic levels?

Fat: Eating ourselves to death? Looks at the complex recipe of modern life that leads to obesity and our options for reversing this trend, from individual to national action. Pocket Issue slims down the issue to give you some answers.

Mary Alexander started her writing career as a journalist before turning to books. She is the author of Calling the Shots, a look at childhood vaccination, Pocket Issue, Food and Pocket Issue, Pandemics, ghost author of the memoir, Call Me Elizabeth.

ISBN: 978-0-9554415-5-4   £6   112 pages   Published: July, 2008

Al Qaeda: the current threat

September 2008

The termination of terrorist training from Afghanistan to the Welsh border; tighter online monitoring of suspects and stronger global terror laws. It seems harder than ever for Al Qaeda to be the force they once were?

On the flip side, stories of fragmented but growing numbers of terror cells springing up throughout North Africa; a new safe haven emerging for terrorists in Pakistan; recruits from some of Europe's most respected universities increasingly willing to sign up to the cause that orchestrated the horrific attacks in New York, London, Madrid. **Pocket Issue** ducks beneath the issue to and asks what is the current threat from Al Qaeda?

Paul Cruickshank, is a fellow at The Center on Law and Security at New York University and a contributor of analysis on Al Qaeda and international security concerns to CNN, the Guardian, the New Republic and The Independent on Sunday.
ISBN: 978-0-9554415-7-8   £6   112 pages   Published: September 2008

Drink & Drugs: culture of excess?

October 2008

Teenagers drinking until they collapse; middle class consumption reaching dangerous levels with record numbers of housewives facing alcohol-induced liver disease; a wrap of cocaine costing less than a trip to the cinema; repeated links between cannabis use and mental health problems. Drinking hours have been extended and cannabis downgraded, while rehabilitation along celebrity lines is expensive and rare on the NHS.

Pocket Issue checks in and asks if there is a quick fix? How is Britain handling societal drugs and alcohol usage? And how does this compare with abroad? Are we so different in our indulgence to the seemingly more civilised Europeans?

Amanda Eleftheriades has written on substance misuse for various publications including The Herald, Big Issue Scotland and Glasgow's Evening Times. She also consults for a number of voluntary and public sector organisations supporting people with drug and alcohol problems.

ISBN: 978-0-9554415-8-5   £6   112 pages   Published: October 2008

Big Brother: who's watching you?

October 2008

Cameras that can see through your clothes at 80 paces; Council tax rising to cover increased CCTV needs; suggestions that Internet Service Providers should monitor customer usage in the comfort of their own homes; plus ID cards, fingerprint and eyeball recognition on the horizon. In the 21st century is there anywhere to hide? And if not, should there be?

Pocket Issue **Big Brother: Who is watching you?** twitches the curtain and takes a hard look at our increasingly hi-tech, zero privacy society.

Joseph O'Neill is a freelance author and broadcaster whose work has featured in all the major family history magazines. He writes a regular feature for the BBC's Who Do You Think You Are? and is author of Crime City, his account of Manchester's Victorian underworld.

ISBN: 978-0-9554415-9-2   £6   112 pages   Published: October 2008

Also from Pocket Issue

Read up on the big global issues with these essential titles from Pocket Issue, and sound knowledgeable when others don't.

Al Qaeda: the current threat

Big Brother: who's watching you?

Drink & Drugs: culture of excess?

The Energy Crisis

Fat: eating ourselfes to death?

Food: what are we really eating?

Global Warming

Middle East Conflict

Pandemics: bird flu, MRSA — should we be worried?

'Precisely what's needed...' Hephzibah Anderson, The Daily Mail

'For everyone who longs to be well-informed but lacks the time (or the attention span)'. Alex Clark, The Observer

Pocket Issue is now available in Audio. Named the Sunday Times Audio Book of the Week, download your free sample at www.talkingissues.com.

Pocket ISSUE
Small briefs for a big world